Vol 8

MAZE

FOR KIDS

Ages 4-6

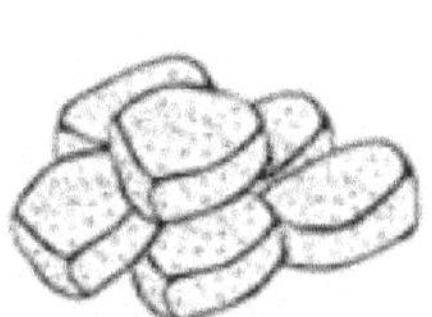

MAZE BOOK

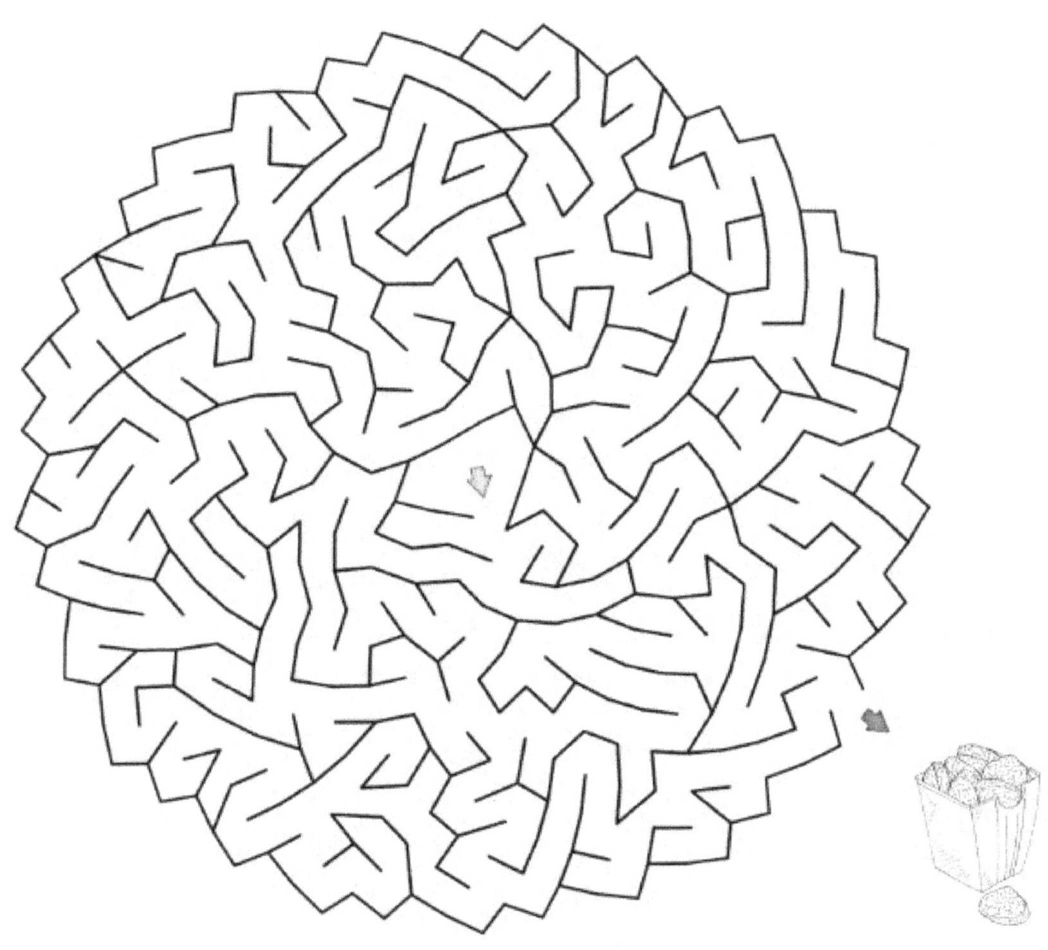

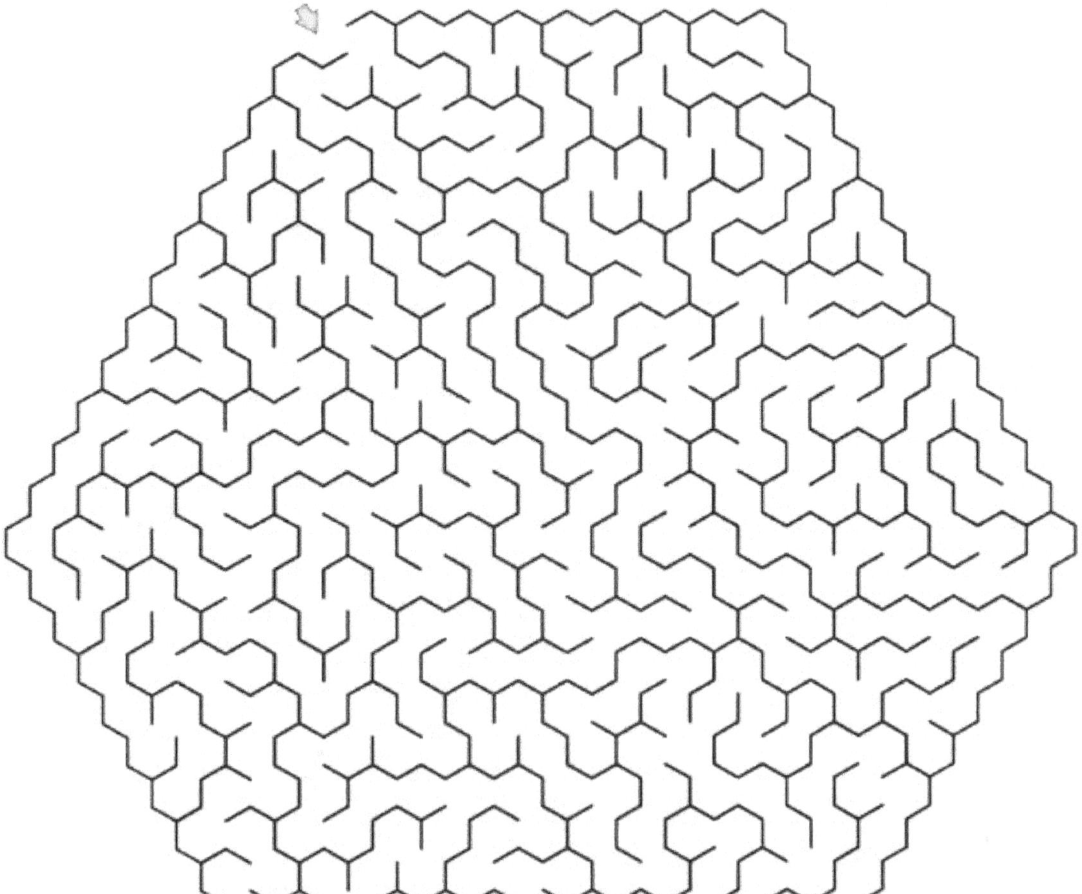

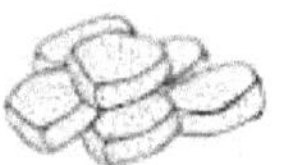

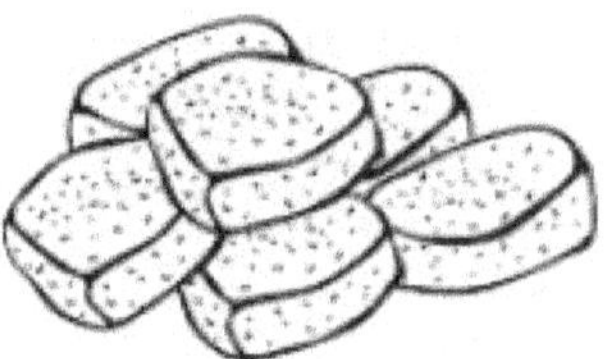

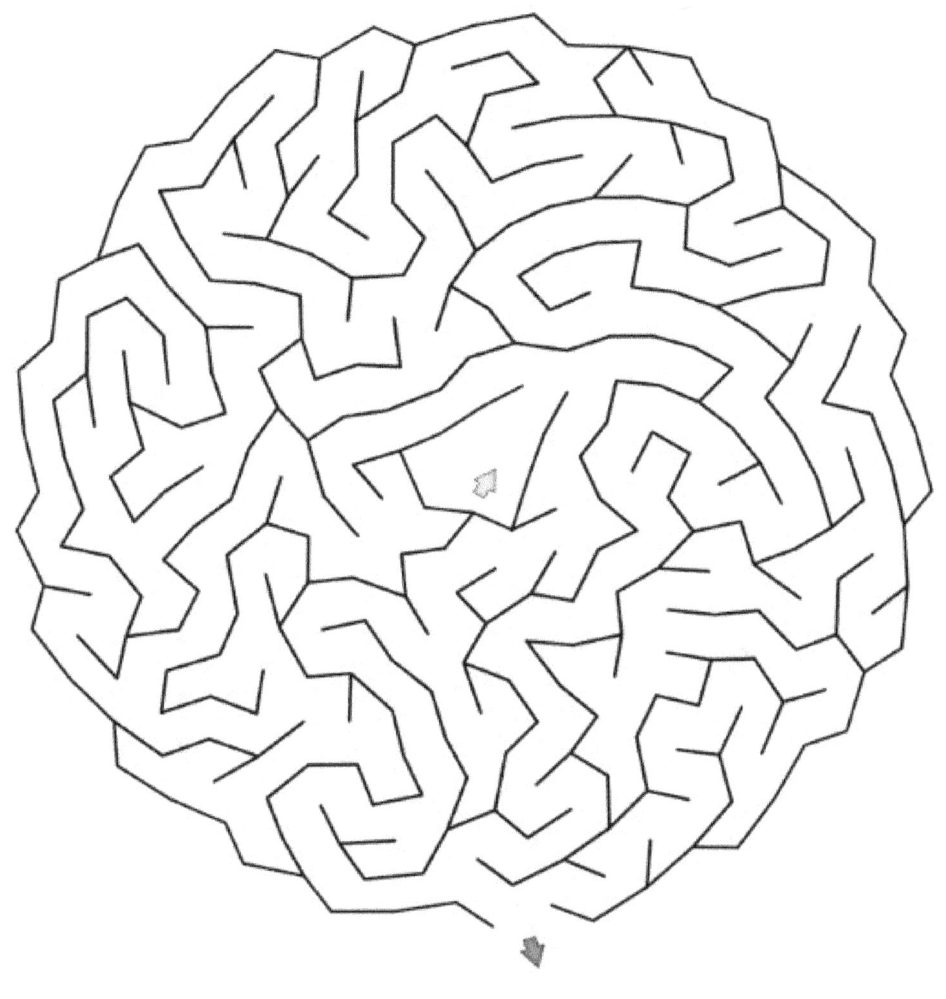

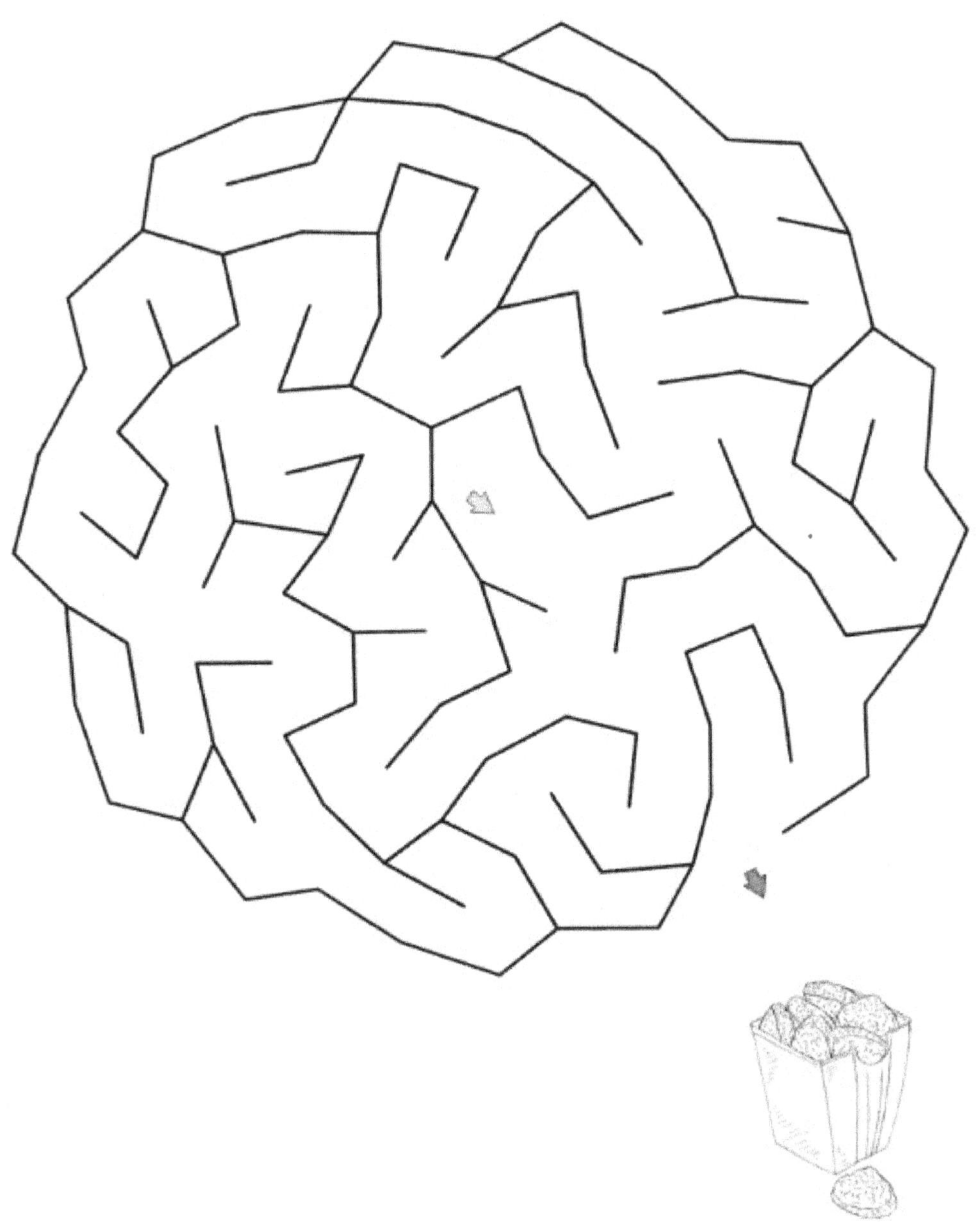

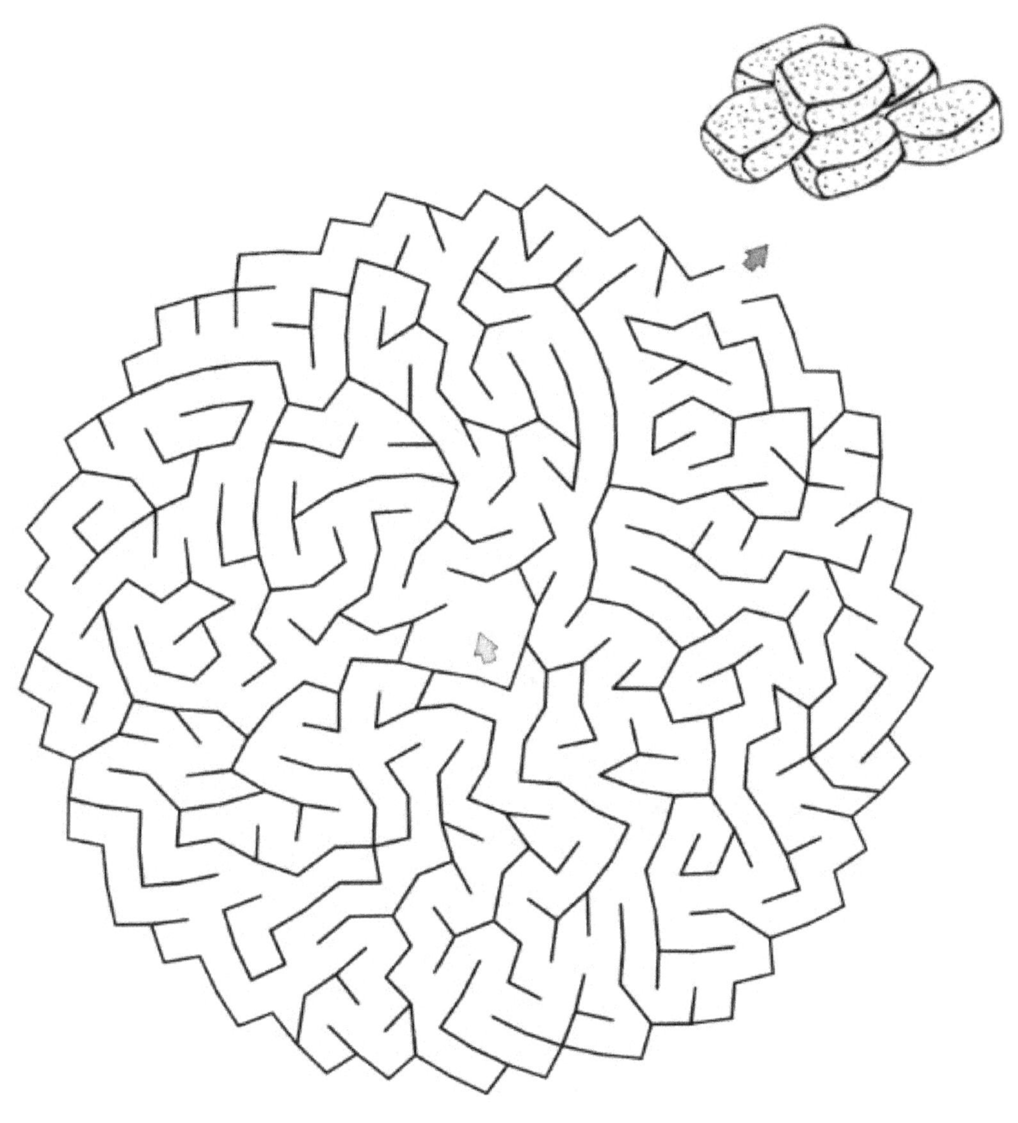

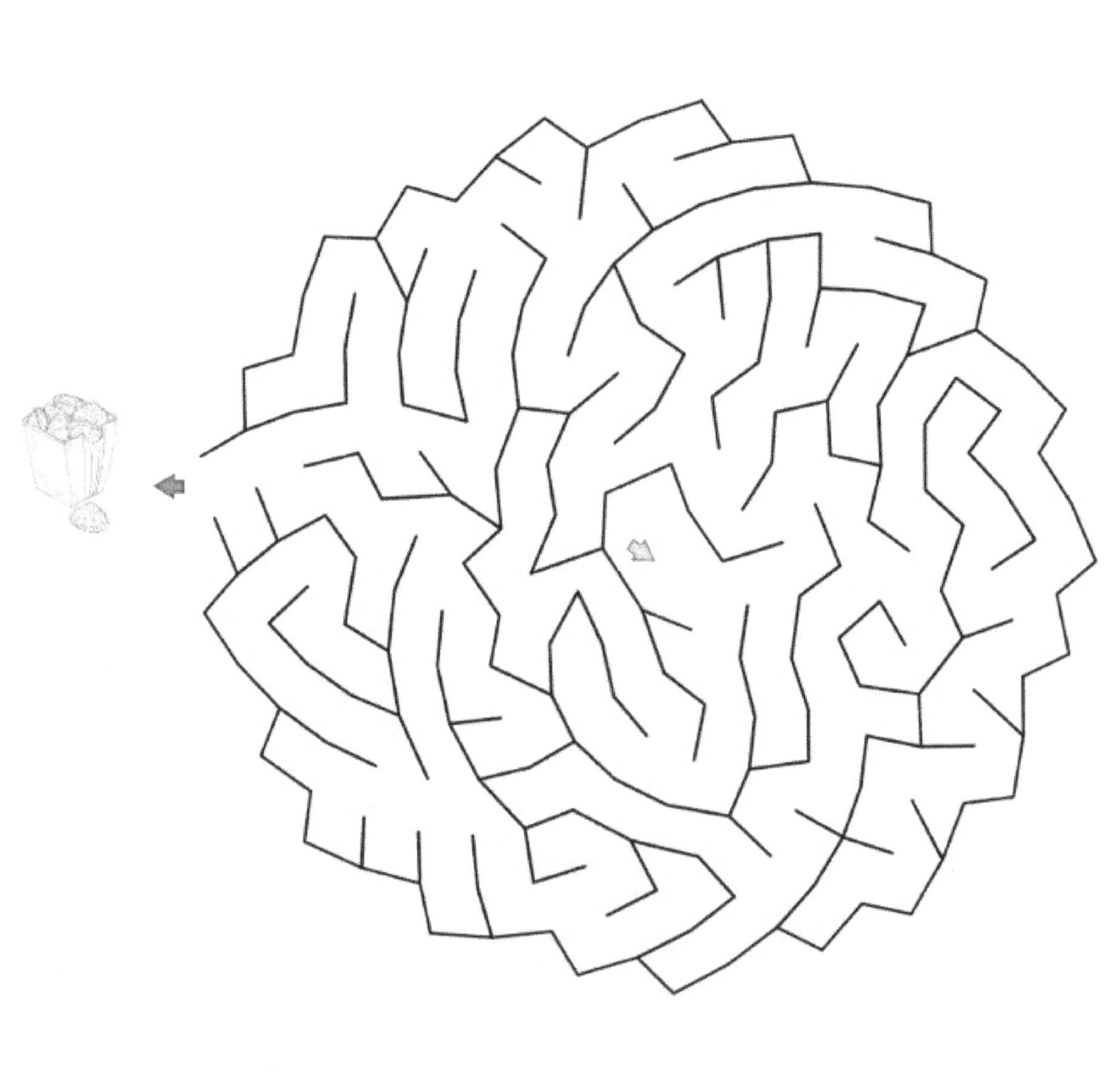

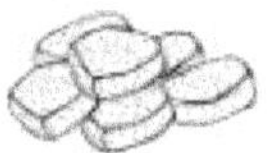

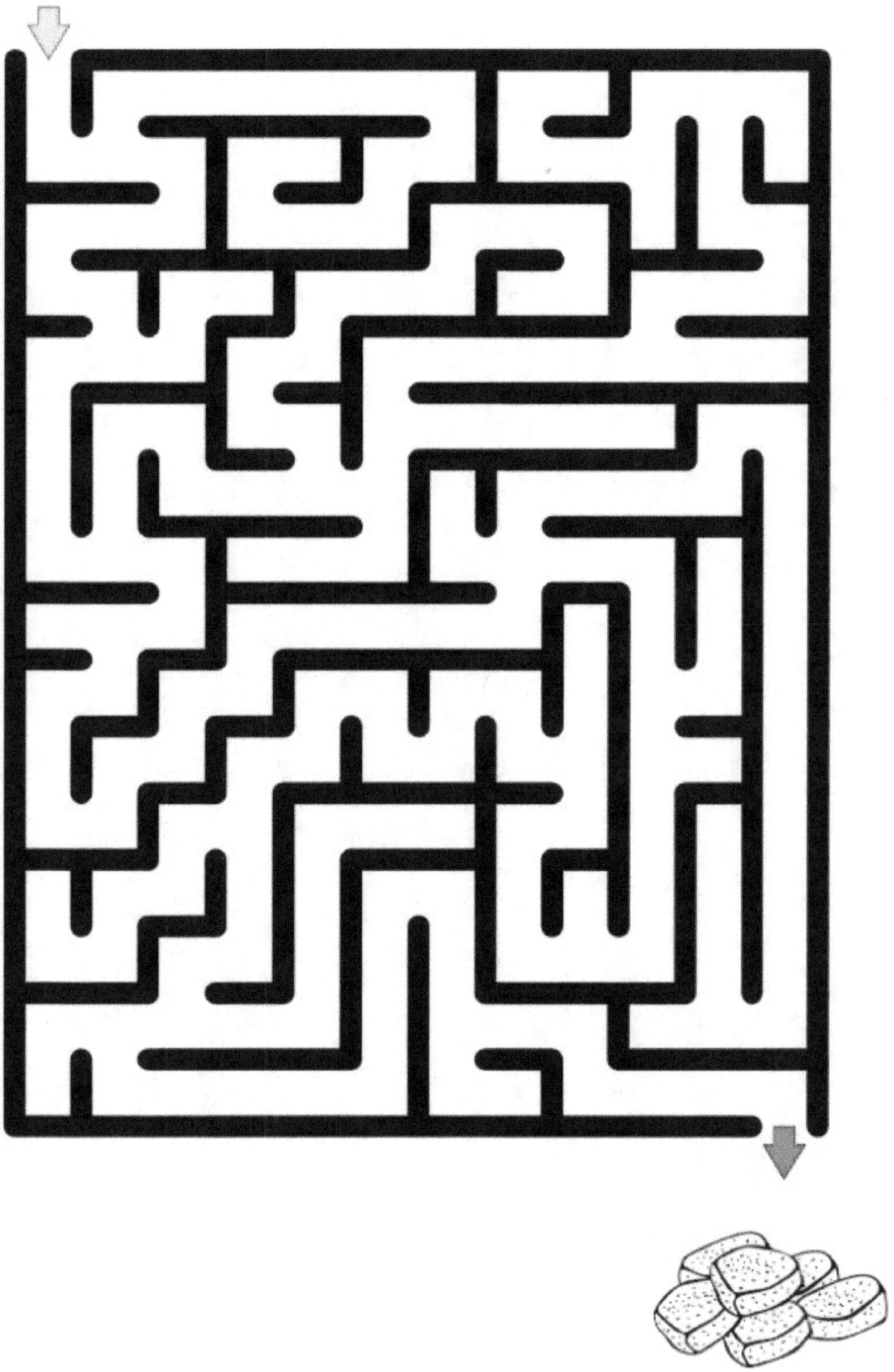

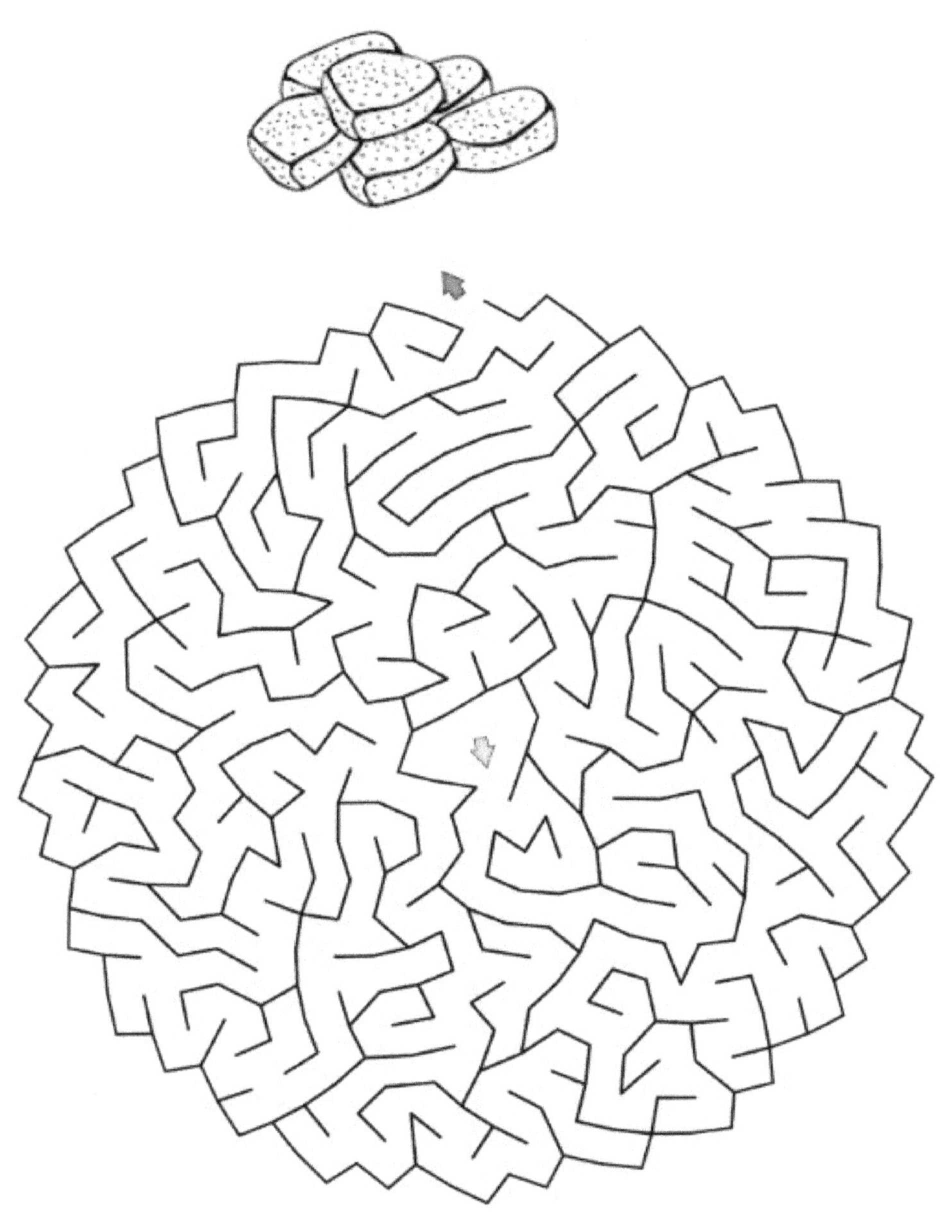

www.ingramcontent.com/pod-product-compliance
Lightning Source LLC
Chambersburg PA
CBHW081736250726
48657CB00010B/3293